Two Treasures

Also by Thich Nhat Hanh in Aleph

Nothing to Do, Nowhere to Go: Waking Up to Who You Are

Good Citizens: Creating Enlightened Society

The Blooming of a Lotus: Essential Guided Meditations for Mindfulness, Healing, and Transformation

The World We Have

Touching Peace: Practising the Art of Mindful Living

Fidelity: How to Create a Loving Relationship That Lasts

Answers from the Heart: Practical responses to Life's Burning Questions

How to Fight

No Mud, No Lotus: The Art of Transforming Suffering

Work: How to Find Joy and Meaning in Each Hour of the Day

Two Treasures

Buddhist Teachings on Awakening and True Happiness

Thich Nhat Hanh

ALEPH

ALEPH

ALEPH BOOK COMPANY
An independent publishing firm
promoted by ***Rupa Publications India***

First published by Parallax Press in 2007.

Published in India in 2023
by Aleph Book Company
7/16 Ansari Road, Daryaganj
New Delhi 110 002

ISBN: 978-81-19635-31-3

1 3 5 7 9 10 8 6 4 2

Printed in India.

CONTENTS

FOREWORD
THE ART OF MINDFULNESS

The very first time Thay (the name by which Thich Nhat Hanh was known to me and many others) spoke to me, it was to ask me to bring the Buddha Dharma back to India. I did not know then how deeply those words would imprint themselves on my mind and give shape and meaning to my life. It was the summer of 1987. I was in Ojai, California, a burned-out activist and seeker who had never even heard of Thich Nhat Hanh. We were a bunch of us organizing an artists' retreat where Thay was to be the guiding teacher, but none of us could pronounce his name so we called it the 'Kick the Can' retreat.

Of course, once he arrived his presence was unforgettable. I stayed in the background, not once speaking to him in the six days he was there, just doing a recording of his talks on a cassette player. But as he was leaving, just as he was about to get into the car, seeing me among the volunteers that had come to say goodbye, our eyes met, and he said: 'Bring the good Buddha Dharma back to India.'

Six months later, when I returned to India, I found myself increasingly interested in Buddhism, gravitating to whichever Buddhist teachers I could find at home. I went on a five-day retreat with the Dalai Lama in Sarnath, and another ten-day retreat led by the Vipassana teacher, S. N. Goenka, in Igatpuri.

This new curiosity about Buddhism led me back to the man I had barely exchanged a word with. Three months after I arrived home, I wrote to Thay, offering to host him in India, should he ever want to visit. I did not even dare expect a reply. But, about a fortnight later, there was a call. It was Sister Chan Khong. Thay wished to come to India to visit the

Buddhist sites, she said, and would I be able to help? Overjoyed, I accepted the offer instantly. Without knowing him, I felt in my bones that he could be the teacher I had been looking for all my life. And this, my chance of a lifetime to be with him.

The only problem was I was clueless on how to organize the trip, I knew almost nothing of the Buddhist pilgrimage route. I had been to some of these sites as a child. But organizing for Thay was another matter. Nevertheless, I set to work. I went on a reconnaissance trip with a friend to all the Buddhist sites, some of which I had never visited before, trying to locate accommodation and book the logistics, including figuring out the route and modes of transport.

It was an exciting but gruelling journey in the middle of India's hottest season in May. As many of the places we were visiting were new to me, I was not quite sure of the distances and modes of public transport. We ended up sleeping on railway platforms, sitting on the roof of buses, eating at odd hours, and being so exhausted that by the time we got to Sravasti, we fell asleep as someone was cooking our lunch and did not wake up for eight hours—in time for dinner instead of lunch.

How different it was when Thay arrived! He came with an entourage of thirty people from different countries, from Argentina to Australia and France to the US. They spent the first three days in Delhi. In my innocence and to keep costs down, I had arranged for their accommodation in the YMCA youth hostel frequented by backpacking tourists from abroad. But Thay and his group were unperturbed, making themselves serenely at home among the backpackers. They even infused the youth hostel with an energy of mindfulness it had never experienced before or since.

The evening after the group landed, I invited Thay to our home. Our home then was a magisterial bungalow, 8, Rajaji Marg, in the centre of New Delhi, allotted to my mother who was then a senior judge at the Delhi High Court. Besides my parents and my brother and sister, I had invited some twenty of my local friends to meet Thay. It was supposed to be one of those tea parties that my mother often hosted but somehow Thay's presence transformed the occasion for everyone there.

As we were having tea in the drawing room, overlooking a large garden, the telephone rang. My mother instantly got up to attend to the call. Thay did not even seem to notice but when she returned from her call, Thay began sharing with us his practice of telephone meditation—the art of stopping and coming back into the present moment each time to the sound of the telephone bell. Turning even the sound of the telephone into a meditation bell.

That tea party was so memorable for the way Thay used every moment as a deep teaching, without appearing to teach at all. On the surface, he was just being social, talking to everyone, but there was not a moment when he ceased teaching.

After tea we went to sit in the garden. It had a pond with purple lilies. I had laid out some cotton carpets, thinking that after our tea, we would sit in the garden to hear Thay teach. But Thay was teaching long before we went into the garden and we didn't even think of it as a teaching. Whether it was inside or outside, Thay sat equally still and his calm communicated itself to us, whether we realized it or not. In the garden, Thay began to share very gently and informally what he had been doing all through the tea party—the art of mindfulness in every moment of our daily lives.

He stood up and all of us got up too. Walking a few gentle steps, he spoke on how to stay mindful of our steps and breath at the same time. Suddenly I was seeing our garden as if for the first time. With each step I could feel the softness of the grass, the coolness of the evening breeze, the magic of the parakeets flying overhead, trees I had not bothered before to distinguish one from another, and so much more. With each step I could feel the energy of Thay's presence. What was even more amazing was to see my parents and siblings—hardened sceptics, all of them—following Thay trustingly on our slow walk across the garden.

There was a beautiful Sita Ashok tree in the garden

that I had not particularly noticed before. Thay stopped near it. It was only later I learnt of the sacredness of the Sita Ashok tree in the Buddhist tradition because the Buddha is believed to have been born under it.

With Thay leading us, I could look more deeply into the trunk, the shapes of the leaves, the colours and the first glimmerings of the realization that even though we could not see the beautiful sunset-coloured flowers of the tree, they would manifest themselves in the right season. And it was not just me. Each of the thirty or more of us in the garden were touched deeply by Thay's simple teaching and walking. Several, including my brother, decided to join for part or the whole of the pilgrimage. My sister had already offered to come anyway just to support me.

I was aware, of course, that Buddhism had pretty much disappeared from India, the land of its birth, but it was during this first pilgrimage with Thay that I discovered how much of the old animosity against Buddhism still persisted.

Thay wanted to start the pilgrimage in Sarnath, as

that is where the Buddha had offered his first teachings. By the time we reached the government guest house in Sarnath our group was tired and in need of a good sleep. But just outside the guesthouse, a tent had been pitched and loud Hindu bhajans were blaring out of it till late at night from discordant speakers. The noise was unbearable. I went across to the tent to try and get them to either switch off the microphones till the morning or at least to reduce the volume. I found just two people in the tent, half asleep, by a cassette recorder and amplifier. I explained to them that there was a community of Buddhist pilgrims across from them who needed their sleep. But my plea to them had an opposite effect. Instead of reducing the volume, they increased it, saying that this was the religion of this land and not Buddhism.

But Thay was teaching us, in his gentle unassuming way how Hinduism and Buddha Dharma are inseparable. When we were in Varanasi, the daily Hindu rituals by the Ganga were very much part of our pilgrimage. Thay made us understand that the

Ganga was not sacred just for Hindus, its sacredness belonged to all spiritual traditions. We were on a rowboat on the Ganga when Thay asked me to sing. I found myself singing a holy chant to the Hindu deity Shiva. Har Har Mahadeva Shambho, Kashi Vishwanath Gange. I closed my eyes and felt the words in sync with my breath. Gradually I speeded it up. In true Hindu tradition, I asked the others to join in as Hindu chanting is always done collectively. It was a lovely feeling of being transported to the other shore as we chanted together on the boat. Thay loved it and over the years would ask me to share the 'Ganges song' whenever I visited Plum Village. It even made its way into the early versions of the Plum Village songbooks.

When we walked into the Deer Park, Thay paused near the entrance to the park and had us gather around. He shared how each step we were making was literally in the footsteps of the Buddha. If we were mindful, we could walk with the awareness of the Buddha and transform our feet into Buddha's feet. As we walked, in a single line, following Thay, it felt like we were walking with the Buddha. Occasionally he would invite a bell, and all of us would stop. We would touch the present moment in a deep way, aware of our breath, the positions of our body, the temperature, the light breeze, the sounds, the colours. All that was within and around us in those moments.

Each day was magical on the pilgrimage. Each day was a profound teaching.

In Bodh Gaya, Thay offered to the Bodhi Tree there a copy of the biography of the Buddha, *Old Path White Clouds*, that he had just completed. We spent a week there, staying at the Vietnamese temple that had just opened. Most days we visited the Mahabodhi temple. We sat under the Bodhi tree, meditated and Thay would teach. Thay had a way of bringing the Buddha alive for us. When he talked of the Buddha it was as if we were under the same tree that the Buddha had sat under 2,600 years ago. He brought alive the Buddha's physical and psychological struggle, the children who became his companions, and the natural vegetation, the tree under which he sat, and the Niranjana River flowing close by. The Buddha's presence shone through Thay, sitting there so calmly, smiling and being totally present. When he looked up at the Bodhi leaves, we saw the Buddha through Thay's eyes and understood how the Buddha had possibly gleaned his deep teachings of inter-being by penetrating the reality of the leaf—the sunshine, the clouds, the earth, the air, and space that had enabled it to manifest.

Each day, we walked meditatively around the temple, attentive to each step, as the Buddha had been. On one side of the temple, there were stones laid down on the path as reminders of each mindful step the Buddha took. But with Thay there, we hardly needed a reminder. Each mindful step we took, he told us, helps others to do the same. With Thay there as our teacher, we were also learning to be co-teachers.

Early one morning, we started on a day-long walk to and from the Dungeshwari caves where the Buddha had practised austerities. Even this became a teaching never to be forgotten—walking along the bunds dividing the rice fields in single file, keeping a space between each other wide enough for a cow to walk through, just how the Buddha and his sangha had walked all those centuries ago. We learned to touch the earth with each step, feeling the 'miracle of walking on earth', to use Thay's favourite phrase.

Each moment was something to be cherished, fully alive and present to whoever and whatever we encountered. As we passed farmers and pastoralists, we stopped and spoke to them about their lives, the rearing of animals and joined some of them in threshing. Children from the villages gathered around us and we occasionally stopped and sat in the shade of a bamboo thicket or large banyan tree, shared tea, and sang songs. Thay picked up a bamboo leaf, and showed the children how to split and roll it so that when they blew through it, it made a sound like a flute.

The children loved Thay. He was their pied piper, and they followed him across the countryside and shallow rivers. His art of telling a story enraptured both the adults and children. One day Thay suggested we gather the children of Bakrour, the village where Sujata had offered the Buddha kheer (rice and milk pudding). We gathered about fifty children between ten and fifteen years old and sat down in a large circle. Thay shared the story of these children's ancestors, Sujata and Svasti, the buffalo boy who had offered the Buddha kusa grass as a meditation asana (cushion). The children listened to these stories with deep attention. Most of them were hearing these stories for the first time. They could see themselves in the story. They moved closer to Thay, some of them clinging to his robes, and he looked at all of them with the eyes of love. Everyone was offered some juice and all the children were taught the practice of drinking mindfully.

By the time, we got to Rajgir, I could see how deeply Thay knew the Buddha and the places associated with his life. Vulture Peak was especially dear to him. When I was making the schedule, he had suggested we spend five days there. I wondered why I had visited the hot springs in Rajgir with my father, as a child, but never Vulture Peak as it was just a hill with nothing there of special interest. But those five days spent at Vulture Peak were truly special, experienced with Thay. Each morning we would climb the hill, often before sunrise and come down after sunset. Walking behind him, as he placed his feet on the same path the Buddha had walked 2,600 years ago, and stopping from time to time to look over the hills and forested landscape unchanged since the Buddha's time, it felt like we were walking with the Buddha, seeing with his eyes. With Thay leading us, it was so easy to feel a deep sense of non-separation with everything within and around us. Watching the sunset each evening as the Buddha had, in silence, gave us a sense of great joy.

An especially memorable day was on 10 November 1988 when Thay ordained the first three monastics in our order. We climbed up to Vulture Peak and all thirty-five of us seated ourselves in a formal arrangement on the flat platform on top of the peak. Thay was in his formal sanghati robe. There was only one other monk from Vietnam, Dr Lam (in whose guest house we had stayed in Bodh Gaya), but it felt as if there was a huge gathering of monastics and lay people, including the Buddha, to witness this historic ceremony.

In his gentle yet solemn way, Thay conducted the ordination ceremony. We were all so moved, and there were tears of joy as Sister Chan Khong, Sister Annabel, and Sister Thanh Minh's heads were shaved. Later, Thay ordained five members into the Order of Interbeing and five others, including me were offered the refuge of the Buddha, Dharma and Sangha, and the five Precepts, as they were called at that time. I was given a Dharma name in Sanskrit by Thay that day, Chitta Bhadra, which Thay translated as Kindness of the Heart.

Our pilgrimage journey had been tough, and some of the living conditions were very basic—there were rats running across our bedrooms in Rajgir. So, when we arrived in Patna, we were all overjoyed to find running hot water, air conditioning, and an excellent restaurant in the hotel we checked into. At least the next three days and nights that we had scheduled in Patna could be spent in comfort. But next morning after breakfast, Thay called me aside to say that he had decided we go on to Vaishali. I was dismayed as it would be impossible to find decent accommodation in Vaishali but Thay was adamant that instead of staying two more nights in Patna, he wanted to move to Vaishali.

Thay was least concerned with creature comforts or accommodation so we left it to the group to choose for themselves whether they wanted to stay back in Patna or risk the limited and basic accommodation available in Vaishali. Finally, only eight of us left for Vaishali. We found only three rooms available in a government guest house there and had to stay three or four to a room.

The first evening in Vaishali, we walked across to the local market. It was near the guest house we were staying in, next to the large coronation tank of the Licchavi kings at the time of the Buddha. At the market there were four or five local farmers who had brought their produce and laid it out on cloth on the earth. Thay loved the ambience and we bought a couple of large fresh gourds to cook for our dinner. One of the farmers we met there invited us to his village, a short fifteen-minute walk away. He and his family, he said, are Buddhists and had been since the Buddha's time. It seemed an unlikely claim, but still, the next day we decided to walk over to the hamlet.

We were welcomed in a most beautiful and touching way. The families were poor and laid out some cloth for us to sit on the earth in front of their homes. They chanted the three refuges and the five precepts in Pali, as the Sri Lankans do and may have taught them. After that our group offered some chants and made some offerings at their small shrine. Thay loved being there and the locals were so happy with our visit that they suggested we start a centre near them. They said they would help in any way and Thay later mentioned to me that we could start a Plum Village centre in Vaishali.

It was an undying dream of Thay's—to start a Plum Village in India. And although a Plum Village centre never happened in Vaishali, we did eventually acquire a piece of land in Dehradun several years later and were able to offer it to Thay and the Plum Village community. When he came to Dehradun in 2008, Thay blessed the piece of land and planted a banyan sapling on it, naming it Plum Village, India.

It would have made Thay happy I think if I had chosen the monastic path. In Kushinagar, when I was sitting under the full moon with Sister Chan Khong and Thay, Sister Chan Khong took a scissors and razor and shaved my head. It seemed quite natural for her to do so since in those days my hair and beard had grown long. A few days later in Lumbini, Nepal, a Theravadan monk offered Thay a robe and he, in turn, offered it to me. I accepted, but I never wore it, and some years later, when in Plum Village, returned it to him. It did not feel the right path for me at the time, and Thay and I discussed it. He felt it was a wonderful path and one that could help many people and was in some ways easier than the path of a householder. I said I needed to experience the role of a householder, earner of a livelihood, a husband and a father, so as to be helpful to others who also have these experiences. Thay said, 'You have to choose.' When I did marry Gitu some years later, he lovingly officiated over our wedding ceremony.

At Lumbini, we visited the Ashokan Pillar with the inscription in the Brahmi script of the third century BCE, mentioning that the Buddha had been born here. Each evening we would sit to share in Dharma discussions, while we stayed at the Garden Guest house. Thay emphasized how each birth was miraculous and if there were the right causes and conditions, as had been at the time of the Buddha, any child had the potential to awaken to be a Buddha.

The pilgrimage was nearly over but not Thay's teaching. We crossed back over the Indo-Nepal border at Bhairava/Sanauli. There was a long row of trucks waiting to get a permit to get across the border creating a massive traffic jam. Fortunately, we were able to edge our way past the trucks as we were a passenger bus and with a few smiles and a lot of patience, had our passports stamped. Thay was always calm, accepting and absorbing things as they were and responding appropriately with just the right amount of energy needed.

The Buddha had spent the most time in Sravasti and Thay enjoyed spending the full days at the Jeta grove. Each day Thay shared stories and teachings like the Anapanasati sutra, offered by the Buddha there. Sometimes we went and sat at the Chinese pagoda temple close by, and invited the large ceremonial bell and drum.

During the pilgrimage, Thay had suggested that if we wanted to give to beggars or wanted to buy something, we should put that money in another pocket. We could decide whom we would like to donate it to when we reached the Jeta Grove in Sravasti, so as to be inspired by the great benefactor of the sangha at the Buddha's time, Anathapindika, who had donated this park to the Buddha and the Sangha.

We knew of a group that was working with the Dalits who had embraced Buddhism, inspired by

Babasaheb Ambedkar. Thay was going to be leading a three-day retreat with them at the Bhaja caves in Maharashtra, after the pilgrimage. As a collective we decided that we would like to support them, the Trailokya Bauddha Mahasangha Sahayaka Gana (TBMSG).

As we closed our pilgrimage circle, 'In the Footsteps of the Buddha', Thay suggested each one of us write an insight poem; one that was inspired by our journey together. It was a lovely way to hear each person's voice and insight.

The pilgrimage was ending but our lives would never quite be the same again. For me it felt as if this was the beginning of a spiritual journey that I am still on. Thay encouraged me to go on the same pilgrimage each year as a practice and invite others to join so that they too can meet the Buddha. Since then, I have been on this pilgrimage—In the Footsteps of the Buddha and Thay—more than a hundred times. I feel blessed to have had this practice suggested to me by Thay, my teacher as each time I get closer to the

Buddha, my spiritual and land ancestor and the living Dharma.

Thay came again to India in 1997, and once more in 2008, under the auspices of the Ahimsa Trust. He was keen to bring the Buddha Dharma back to the land of its birth, where it had pretty much disappeared since the thirteenth century CE.

This was a deep volition in him and he could see that I could support and continue this mission. On both these subsequent trips we visited some of the pilgrimage places, but Thay's emphasis was on sharing the Buddha's teachings and practices with as many people as he could from this land of his teacher that he loved so much.

By 1997, some of his books, including *Old Path White Clouds* had been translated into Hindi, and he shared the Buddha's spiritual teachings and practice in Delhi (India International Centre, Rajiv Gandhi Foundation), Kolkata (Ladies Club), and Chennai (The Theosophical Society). It was on this visit that he had a memorable meeting with the then vice president of India who later became the president, K. R. Narayanan. Thay was able to impress upon Narayanan who was the chairman of the Rajya Sabha the vital need for ethics in politics and soon after this meeting, a Committee on Ethics was set up in the Indian parliament. Thay was also keen that we set up an active sangha in India, which we did, mainly in the Delhi area and in Kolkata.

By 2008, when Thay came again, he was much better known and the Government of India invited him as a state guest under the Distinguished Visitor's programme of the Indian Council of Cultural Relations (ICCR) and to deliver the Gandhi Memorial Lecture.

To reach as many people as possible, Ahimsa Trust collaborated with several prestigious organizations. Thay offered special sessions for educators, the media, scholars, business leaders, parliamentarians, doctors, religious leaders and children, besides the general public. He also reached out to many disadvantaged people of India, including the Dalits and youthful Shakyas in Sankasiya. He offered retreats at Teen

Murti Bhavan in New Delhi, The Doon School in Dehradun, and Nagaloka in Nagpur. Thay attracted national attention during his visit, as he encouraged efforts to bring mindfulness into the mainstream. The visit was covered by the national media. In fact, the walking meditation he led on Raj Path on Gandhi Jayanti was carried in every single paper in Delhi and a host of national TV channels.

I was in Kushinagar, where the Buddha passed away, on the night of 11 November 2014 when I heard that Thay had suffered a massive stroke. Over the next days and weeks, it was uncertain that he would survive. I went to visit him in the hospital in France over Christmas, and though extremely weak, he held my hand and smiled. Miraculously, Thay revived and with excellent medical support and deeply compassionate care he lived on, but could not speak again and was confined to a wheelchair.

However, his presence was very strong. When

Gitu and I visited him in Thailand, he looked deeply into her eyes and then my eyes for a long period, transmitting without words, deep into our being.

Thay was determined to return to Vietnam and live the last phase of his life there at the Tu Hieu monastery in Hue where he had been ordained and was the de facto abbot.

When I awoke on 22 January 2022 I saw a message from the Abbot of Plum Village, 'Our teacher is now free as a cloud.'

Thay had passed away peacefully at midnight at our root temple in Hue. It felt that Thay was free as the Buddha was many centuries ago. There are not many who are able to transcend the constraints and concepts of birth and death. Thay had shown us the path of awakening as a human being, of being the white cloud in the blue sky, and he always carried the confidence in us, his students, that we have that potential too.

With great wisdom and compassion, he taught us moment by moment for decades and built a global sangha. Thay dearly loved India, the home of his own teacher, the Buddha, and many of us were blessed by his presence and practice when he visited India in 1988, 1997, and 2008.

His presence and teaching touched the lives of countless Indians and he continues in all of us in India who were fortunate to have known, heard, and read him. His lineage continues in many schools, in the police, in the many sanghas in the Plum Village tradition. He has helped cultivate and renew the branch of Engaged Buddhism in the land of its birth in a way that is accessible and appropriate to our times.

Dharmacharya Shantum Seth

INTRODUCTION

When I was seventeen and in my first year of novice studies at a Buddhist monastery in Vietnam, I had to memorize the *Sutra on the Eight Realizations of the Great Beings* and the *Discourse on Happiness*. Over sixty years have passed, and I still find these two texts to be torches that help light my path.

In 1978, I became involved in a project to rescue Vietnamese boat people in the South China Sea. We printed the Sutra on the Eight Realizations of the Great Beings in a small booklet in Vietnamese to help the survivors as they found a new home somewhere in the world. Soon, we found this sutra, as well as the Discourse on Happiness, to be very helpful for those in the West as well. All of us, whatever our past experiences, are struggling to find happiness and realize full consciousness in our daily lives.

I invite you to read this book at a time when your body and mind are completely relaxed, for example after taking a comfortable bath. You can light a candle or a stick of incense to give the room a pleasant glow or fragrance. Then, read one of these sutras slowly to discover its deepest meaning. These sutras are thousands of years old, but it is only by relating them to your own life's experience that they come alive and you can understand them.

The more you meditate on these sutras, the more deeply you will discover the profound wisdom they contain. The two sutras in this book complement each other. They can be read separately, but together they explain in practical detail how to progress step-by-step toward awakening and happiness.

Thich Nhat Hanh
July 2006

THE SUTRA ON THE EIGHT REALIZATIONS OF THE GREAT BEINGS[1]

Wholeheartedly, day and night, a disciple of the Buddha should recite and meditate on the eight realizations discovered by the great beings.

The First Realization is the awareness that the world is impermanent. All political regimes are subject to fall; all things composed of the four elements are empty and contain the seeds of suffering[2]. Human beings are composed of five *skandha* (aggregates) and are without a separate self[3]. They are always in the process of change—constantly being born and constantly dying. They are empty of self, without sovereignty. The mind is the source of all confusion, and the body is the forest of all impure actions. If we meditate on these facts, we can gradually be released from *samsara,* the round of birth and death.

The Second Realization is the awareness that more desire brings more suffering. All hardships in daily life arise from greed and desire. Those with little desire and ambition are able to relax, their bodies and minds free from entanglement.

The Third Realization is that the human mind is always searching for possessions and never feels fulfilled. This causes impure actions to ever increase. Bodhisattvas, however, always remember the principle of having few desires[4]. They live a simple life in peace in order to practice the Way, and consider the realization of perfect understanding as their only career.

The Fourth Realization is the awareness of the extent to which laziness is an obstacle to practice. For this reason, we must practice diligently to destroy the unwholesome mental factors that bind us, and to conquer the four kinds of Mara[5], in order to free ourselves from the prisons of the five aggregates and the three worlds[6].

The Fifth Realization is the awareness that ignorance is the cause of the endless round of birth and death. Therefore, bodhisattvas always remember to listen and learn in order to develop their understanding and eloquence. This enables them to educate living beings and bring them to the realm of great joy.

The Sixth Realization is the awareness that poverty creates hatred and anger, which creates a vicious cycle of negative thoughts and activity. When practicing generosity, bodhisattvas consider everyone, friends and enemies alike, as equal. They do not condemn anyone's past wrongdoings, nor do they hate those who are presently causing harm.

The Seventh Realization is that the five categories of desire lead to difficulties[7]. Although we are in the world, we should try not to be caught up in worldly matters. A monk, for example, has in his possession only three robes and one bowl. He lives simply in order to practice the Way. His precepts keep him free of attachment to worldly things, and he treats everyone equally and with compassion.

The Eighth Realization is the awareness that the fire of birth and death is raging, causing endless suffering everywhere. We should take the Great Vow to help everyone, to suffer with everyone, and to guide all beings to the realm of great joy.

These eight realizations are the discoveries of great beings, buddhas, and bodhisattvas who have diligently practiced the way of compassion and understanding. They have sailed the *Dharmakaya*[8] boat to the shore of nirvana, but then they return to the ordinary world, having abandoned the five desires, with their minds and hearts directed toward the noble way, using these eight realizations to help all beings recognize the suffering in this world[9]. If the disciples of the Buddha recite these eight realizations and meditate on them, they will put an end to countless misunderstandings and difficulties and progress toward enlightenment, leaving behind the world of birth and death, dwelling forever in peace.

COMMENTARY ON THE SUTRA ON THE EIGHT REALIZATIONS OF THE GREAT BEINGS

The most accessible way to approach the Sutra on the Eight Realizations of the Great Beings is to see each of the eight items discussed as a subject of meditation. In addition, there are eleven guidelines for daily living that can be found in the sutra. Although the form of the sutra is simple, its content is extremely profound and marvellous. This sutra is not an analytical treatise or a historical artifact; it's a realistic and effective approach to meditation and a guide for our interactions with others.

THE FIRST REALIZATION

The first realization explains and clarifies the four basic subjects of Buddhist meditation: impermanence, suffering, no-self, and impurity. We must always remember and meditate on these four principles of reality. As mentioned in the sutra, if someone meditates on these facts, she will gradually be released from samsara, the round of birth and death.

Impermanence

This refers to the transient nature of all things. From moment to moment, all things in this world, including human life, mountains, rivers, political systems, are in constant transformation. This is called impermanence in each moment. Everything passes through a period of birth, maturity, transformation, and destruction. This destruction is called impermanence in each cycle. To see the impermanent nature of all things, we must examine this closely. Doing so will prevent us from being imprisoned by the things of this world.

Suffering

Suffering has to do with the emptiness of all things. The ancient people of India said that all things are composed of four elements: earth, air, water, and fire. Acknowledging this, buddhas and bodhisattvas understand that when there is a harmonious relationship among the four elements, there is peace. When the four elements are not in harmony, there is suffering.

Because all things are created by a combination of these elements, nothing can exist independently or permanently. All things are impermanent. Consequently, when we are caught up in the things of the world, we suffer from their impermanent nature. And since all things are empty, when we are caught by things, we also suffer from their emptiness. Awareness of the existence of suffering leads us to begin to practice the way of realization. This is the first of the Four Noble Truths[10]. When we lose awareness of and do not meditate on the existence of suffering in all things, we can easily be pushed around by passions and desires for worldly things, increasingly destroying our lives in the pursuit of these desires. Only by being aware of suffering can we find its cause, confront it directly, and eliminate it.

SELFLESSNESS (NO-SELF)

Buddhism teaches that human beings are composed of five aggregates, called skandhas in Sanskrit. If the form created by the four elements is empty and without self, then human beings, created by the unification of the five skandhas, must also be empty and without self. Human beings are involved in a transformation process from second to second, minute to minute, continually experiencing impermanence in each moment. By looking very deeply into the five skandhas, we can experience the selfless nature of our bodies, our passage through birth and death, and emptiness, thereby destroying the illusion that our bodies are permanent. In Buddhism, no-self is the most important subject for meditation. By meditating on no-self, we can break through the barrier between self and other. When we no longer are separate from the universe, a completely harmonious existence with the universe is created. We see that all other human beings exist in us and that we exist in all other human beings. We see that the past and the future are contained in the present moment, and we can penetrate and be completely liberated from the cycle of birth and death.

Modern science has also discovered the truth of the selfless nature of all things. The approach of British biologist Lyall Watson, for example, corresponds entirely with the principle of dependent origination and no-self[41]. Scientists who meditate continuously on the selfless nature of their own bodies and minds, as well as the selfless nature of all things, will one day easily attain enlightenment.

IMPURITY

In terms of the nature of our bodies and minds, impurity means the absence of an immaculate state of being, one that is neither holy nor beautiful. From the Buddhist psychological and physiological standpoint, all human beings are impure. This is not a negative judgment, but an objective perspective on human beings. If we examine the constituents of our bodies from the hair on our head to the blood, pus, phlegm, excrement, urine, the many bacteria dwelling in the intestines, and the many diseases present waiting for the opportunity to develop, it seems clear that our bodies are impure and subject to decay. Our bodies also create the motivation to pursue the satisfaction of our desires and passions. That is why the sutra regards the body as the place where misdeeds gather.

Similarly, the mind is the place where misunderstandings gather. Since we are unable to see the truth of impermanence, suffering, and the selfless nature of all things, our minds often become the victims of greed and hatred, and we act as if we are individual isolated beings who will live forever. So the sutra says, "The mind is the source of all confusion."

THE SECOND REALIZATION

"More desire brings more suffering" is the basis of the second realization. Most people define happiness as the satisfaction of all desires. There are five types of desire[12]. These desires are boundless but our ability to realize them is not, and unfulfilled desires always create suffering. When desires are only partially fulfilled, we continue to pursue their complete fulfillment, and we create more suffering. Even when a desire is fulfilled, we suffer when its fulfillment terminates. It is only after we become completely exhausted from this incessant pursuit that we begin to realize the extent to which we were caught in the insatiable net of desires and passions. Then we can realize that true happiness is really a peaceful state of body and mind, and this can only exist when our desires are few. Having few desires and not seeking fulfillment through the pursuit of the five desires arc great steps toward liberation.

THE THIRD REALIZATION

Knowing how to feel satisfied with few possessions destroys desire and greed. This means being content with material conditions that allow us to be healthy and strong enough to practice the Way. This is an effective way to cut through the net of passions and desires, attain a peaceful state of body and mind, have more time to help others, and be free to realize the highest goal: the development of concentration and understanding to attain realization. Knowing how to feel satisfied with few possessions helps us avoid buying unnecessarily and becoming part of an economic system that exploits others, and it enables us to decrease our involvement in the pollution of our environment.

THE FOURTH REALIZATION

Diligent practice destroys laziness. After we cease looking for joy in desires and passions and know how to feel satisfied with few possessions, we must not be lazy, letting days and months slip by neglectfully. Great patience and diligence are needed continually to develop our concentration and understanding in the endeavor of self-realization. We must use all of our time to meditate on the four truths of impermanence, suffering, selflessness, and impurity, the first four subjects of meditation. We must penetrate deeply into the profound meaning of The Four Foundations of Mindfulness[13], practicing, studying, and meditating on the postures and cycles (becoming, maturing, transformation, and destruction) of our bodies as well as our feelings, sensations, mental formations, and consciousness. We should read sutras and other writings that explain meditation, correct sitting, and controlling the breath, such as the Satipatthana Sutta and The Mahaprajnaparamita Heart Sutra. We have to follow the teachings of these sutras and practice them in an intelligent way, choosing the methods that best apply to our own situation. As necessary, we can modify the methods suggested in order to accommodate our own needs. Our energy must also be regulated until all the basic desires and passions—greed, anger, narrow-mindedness, arrogance, doubt, and preconceived ideas—are uprooted. At this time we will know that our bodies and minds are liberated from the imprisonment of birth and death, the five skandhas, and the three worlds.

THE FIFTH REALIZATION

Concentration and understanding destroy narrow-mindedness. Among the basic desires and passions, narrow-mindedness has the deepest roots. When these roots are loosened, all other desires and passions—greed, anger, doubt, and preconceived ideas—are also uprooted. Knowing this, we can make a great effort to meditate on the truths of impermanence, no-self, and the dependent origination of all things. Once the roots of ignorance are severed, we can liberate ourselves and teach others to break through the chains of birth and death.

The first four subjects of meditation are to help us attain liberation. The next four subjects have the aim of helping others attain liberation, thus clearly and solidly uniting Theravada and Mahayana Buddhist thought.

THE SIXTH REALIZATION

Every person, no matter what their wealth, is equally capable of practicing generosity. Some people think that they can practice generosity only if they are wealthy. This isn't true. Some people who are very wealthy do practice generosity, but many only do charity with the aim of gaining merit, profiting, or pleasing others. People whose lives are grounded in compassion are seldom rich because they share whatever they have with others. They are not willing to enrich their lives financially at the cost of others' poverty. Many people misunderstand the Buddhist expression "practicing generosity" to mean casually giving five or ten cents to a beggar on the street if we happen to have it in our pockets.

The practice of generosity is more beautiful than that. It is both modest and grand. Practicing generosity means continually acting in a way that will help equalize the difference between the wealthy and the impoverished. Whatever we do to ease human suffering and create social justice can be considered practicing generosity. That is not to say that we must become active in any political system. To engage in partisan political action that leads to a power struggle among opposing parties and causes death and destruction is not what we mean by practicing generosity.

How can a person practicing "knowing how to feel satisfied with few possessions" also practice generosity? It is by living simply. Almost everyone who spends his or her life serving and helping others, sacrificing themselves for the sake of humanity, lives simply. If they live their lives worrying about making money and gaining merit, how can they practice generosity? Mahatma Gandhi lived a very simple life; nevertheless his merit helping humanity and saving human beings was immeasurable. There are thousands of people among us who live very simply, while being very helpful to many, many others. They do not have as great a reputation as Gandhi, but their merit is no less than his. It is enough for us just to be a little more attentive and aware of the presence of people like these. They do not practice generosity by giving money that they do not possess, but rather by giving their time, energy, love, and care—their entire lives.

Practicing generosity in a Buddhist context means to consider everyone equal, not to discriminate against anyone. There are cruel persons and kind persons among the poor and destitute, just as there are among the wealthy, and we must not exclude the cruel ones from our practice.

As the sutra states, "Bodhisattvas consider everyone, friends and enemies alike, as equal. They do not condemn anyone's past wrongdoings, nor do they hate those who are presently doing harm." This expresses the spirit of Mahayana Buddhism. Poverty creates anger, hatred, and wrongdoing. If we teach Buddhist philosophy though lectures, but do not practice generosity to ease the suffering of others, we have not yet attained the essence of Buddhism. We should practice generosity with compassion and not disdain, without discriminating against people who, because of their poverty, have caused anger and hatred.

THE SEVENTH REALIZATION

While living in society, we should not be defiled by it. We must live in harmony with society in order to help others, without being caught by the five desires, living like the lotus flower that blooms in the mud and yet remains pure and unstained. Practicing the way of liberation does not mean avoiding society, but helping in it. Before our capacity to help becomes strong and solid, we may be defiled by living in society. For this reason, bodhisattvas meditate on the detrimental nature of the five desires and firmly decide to live simply in order to practice generosity without discrimination. Thus, living in society and not being stained by it is to practice the *six paramitas.* Paramita means to help others reach the other shore, the shore of liberation from sickness, poverty, hunger, ignorance, desires and passions, and birth and death. The six paramitas are: giving, observing the precepts, using diligent effort, endurance, concentration, and understanding.

THE EIGHTH REALIZATION

We should create in ourselves the firm decision to help others. We must make a deep and solemn vow to overcome the difficulties, dangers, and suffering that may occur while helping others. Since the suffering in society is limitless, the willingness and devotion to practice the way of helping others must also be limitless. Thus, the Mahayana spirit is an endless source of energy that inspires us to practice generosity without discrimination. With the Mahayana spirit, we can withstand the many challenges and humiliations encountered in society and are able to continue to practice the Way. This will bring great happiness to others.

ELEVEN GUIDELINES FOR DAILY LIFE

The Mahayana Buddhist practice of the six paramitas is, in part, inspired by this sutra.

The Sutra on the Eight Realizations of the Great Beings is a great resource for meditation. But it is not intended for us to simply meditate on this sutra and then to continue living our lives as before. To fully benefit from this sutra, we must also practice and observe its teachings. Here are eleven guidelines for daily life, based on the insights found in the sutra:

1

While meditating on the body, do not hope or pray to be exempt from sickness. Without sickness, desires and passions can easily arise.

2

While acting in society, do not hope or pray not to have any difficulties. Without difficulties, arrogance can easily arise.

3

While meditating on the mind, do not hope or pray not to encounter hindrances. Without hindrances, present knowledge will not be challenged or broadened.

4

While working, do not hope or pray not to encounter obstacles. Without obstacles, the vow to help others will not deepen.

5

While developing a plan, do not hope or pray to achieve success easily. With easy success, arrogance can easily arise.

6

While interacting with others, do not hope or pray to gain personal profit. With the hope for personal gain, the spiritual nature of the encounter is diminished.

7

While speaking with others, do not hope or pray not to be disagreed with. Without disagreement, self-righteousness can flourish.

8

While helping others, do not hope or pray to be paid. With the hope of remuneration, the act of helping others will not be pure.

9

If you see personal profit in an action, do not participate in it. Even minimal participation will stir up desires and passions.

10

When wrongly accused, do not attempt to exonerate yourself. Attempting to defend yourself will create needless anger and animosity.

11

The Buddha spoke of sickness and suffering as effective medicines. Times of difficulties and accidents are also times of freedom and realization. Obstacles can be a form of liberation. The Buddha reminded us that the army of evil can be the guards of the Dharma. Difficulties are required for success. The person who mistreats one can be one's good friend. One's enemies are as an orchard or garden. The act of doing someone a favor can be as base as the act of casting away a pair of old shoes. The abandonment of material possessions can be wealth and being wrongly accused can be the source of strength to work for justice.

THE DISCOURSE ON HAPPINESS

I heard these words of the Buddha one time when the Lord was living in the vicinity of Savatthi at the Anathapindika Monastery in the Jeta Grove. Late at night, a deva appeared whose light and beauty made the whole Jeta Grove shine radiantly. After paying respects to the Buddha, the deva asked him a question in the form of a verse:

> "Many gods and men are eager to know
> what are the greatest blessings
> which bring about a peaceful and happy life.
> Please, Tathagata, will you teach us?"

(This is the Buddha's answer):
"Not to be associated with the foolish ones,
To live in the company of wise people,
Honoring those who are worth honoring—
This is the greatest happiness.

"To live in a good environment,
To have planted good seeds
And to realize that you are on the right path—
This is the greatest happiness.

"To have a chance to learn and grow,
To be skillful in your profession or craft,
Practicing the precepts and loving speech—
This is the greatest happiness.

"To be able to serve and support your parents,
To cherish your own family,
To have a vocation that brings you joy—
This is the greatest happiness.

"To live honestly, generous in giving,
To offer support to relatives and friends,
Living a life of blameless conduct—
This is the greatest happiness.

"To avoid unwholesome actions,
Not caught by alcoholism or drugs,
And to be diligent in doing good things—
This is the greatest happiness.

"To be humble and polite in manner,
To be grateful and content with a simple life,
Not missing the occasion to learn the
Dharma—
This is the greatest happiness.

"To persevere and be open to change,
To have regular contact with monks and nuns,
And to fully participate in Dharma
discussions—
This is the greatest happiness.

"To live diligently and attentively,
To perceive the Noble Truths,
And to realize nirvana—
This is the greatest happiness.

"To live in the world
With your heart undisturbed by the world,
With all sorrows ended, dwelling in peace—
This is the greatest happiness.

"For the one who accomplishes this
Is unvanquished wherever she goes;
Always he is safe and happy—
Happiness lives within oneself."

COMMENTARY ON THE DISCOURSE ON HAPPINESS

The pali version of this sutra is called the Mangala Sutta[14]. *Mangala* means a good omen, a forewarning of something to come, usually something positive that will bring happiness and prosperity. The word also connotes a blessing because in this sutra the Buddha teaches about the most important blessings, those things that bring happiness.

As with the Sutra on the Eight Realizations of the Great Beings, this sutra can be broken down, stanza by stanza, for meditation, as well as reflected on as a whole. For ease, each stanza is repeated below, followed by the related commentary.

"Not to be associated with the foolish ones,
To live in the company of wise people,
Honoring those who are worth honoring—
This is the greatest happiness."

The greatest blessing is to have good, wise, kind-hearted friends close by. We can't be happy unless we have a sane, healthy space within us and around us. We need a habitat that is beautiful and nourishing, and that gives us the safety and the freedom that we need.

It is a great blessing to be among brothers, sisters, and friends who are practicing kindness and refraining from violence, stealing, and cruelty, and not caught up in addiction to alcohol, drugs, or gambling.

A community that practices love and understanding is the best antidote to addiction to drugs, alcohol, and casual and careless sex. When people suffer, they look for these distractions in order to forget their pain. But these things only distract us temporarily from our suffering, they don't heal us.

Our community can be a family that sustains us. We can't handpick everybody with whom we interact in our daily life, but we can chose to live among those who are kind and virtuous. When we can interact with those who are honorable and have great virtue, we are creating conditions that will bring us lasting happiness.

> *"To live in a good environment,*
> *To have planted good seeds*
> *And to realize that you are on the right path—*
> *This is the greatest happiness."*

"To live in a good environment," means to live in a place where the surroundings and all the activities have the purpose of nourishing us and building community. Without this base environment, we can't go very far. When we practice meditation together, eat together, or work together in a loving and aware way, we are nourishing our peace and harmony.

The physical environment and the presence of others is very important. Often, if we are home alone, even sitting for fifteen minutes of meditation seems impossible. We think we have so many other things to do, or perhaps we feel silly sitting alone like that. But if everyone around us is sitting, we find it much easier! That's why creating a nourishing environment is crucial. Only with this support, can we be a source of joy for ourselves and others.

Community—called *Sangha* in Buddhism—and time are the two ingredients of the universal medicine. If you can take that medicine every day for a number of years, then you have a chance. You become a plant, a tree, deeply rooted in the soil of the Sangha. Happiness and love become possible. And then you can go back and help your own blood family, your own spiritual community, and your society.

It's crucial that we all learn the art of Sangha building and figure out how to create a nourishing, harmonious environment in our lifetime. If we do not have this base, then there is nothing to keep us on the right path and keep us from entering the hell realms or the realm of the hungry ghosts. We don't need to leave this Earth to look for hell. Hell realms are everywhere, even in the town in which we live.

There are hell realms that we have visited, or that we have lived through, and we know that these hell realms are real. We may have been caught in situations of abuse, violence, cruelty, fear, or addiction. We may have been carried away by strong emotions, such as hatred, jealousy, or infatuation, and so committed unwholesome actions. And we know that all over the world countless living beings are suffering in situations of war, poverty, injustice, and environmental destruction.

Hungry ghosts are demons who are perpetually craving food but are unable to take in nourishment. Hungry ghosts are not a myth—they live among us as people who may have enough food and clothing but who are still hungry for knowledge, for love, for hope, and for something to believe in. We have to build community a little bit everywhere so these hungry ghosts can find refuge. It is the atmosphere of harmony and community that can help the hungry ghosts get rooted and undo their knots of suffering.

With our nourishing community around us, we can find the right path to stability, ease, and liberation. Having a path is wonderful. Seeing the path is already great happiness. There is no reason to be fearful or confused anymore. Once we have recognized the path, our sense of loss, confusion, and despair dissipate. Happiness becomes immediately possible.

> *"To have a chance to learn and grim,*
> *To be skillful in your profession or craft,*
> *Practicing the precepts and loving speech—*
> *This is the greatest happiness."*

"To have a chance to learn and grow," means to have the opportunity to have a good education as well as to learn the Dharma. Learning is something that must happen every day, even for the Buddha! We want to have a vocation that does not cause harm to others or to the environment. When we can learn and practice our skills at the same time we support ourselves and our families, this is already a great blessing. There are many lucrative vocations that keep us twisting and turning in bed at night because they are not ethical. Those vocations cause harm to others or to the environment, and they force us to lie and hide the truth. Even though these jobs may be lucrative, they cause us a lot of suffering, suffering that goes deep into our soul. When we are able to find a job that expresses our ideal of compassion, happiness arises, even if the job is not as lucrative. Having a vocation that does not cause harm to others, to the environment, and through which we can express our compassion is a cause for great happiness.

Two thousand five hundred years ago, the Buddha offered his lay students five precepts or guidelines to help them live a peaceful, wholesome, and happy life. We call them the Five Mindfulness Trainings. Mindfulness—the awareness of what is going on in our body, our feelings, our mind, and in the world—is the basis of each training. With mindfulness, we can avoid harming ourselves and others, we protect ourself, our family, and our society, and we ensure safety and happiness now and in the future.

Even if we are happy in our work and following the precepts, it still requires daily commitment to practice loving speech and refrain from speaking to others with harsh words. When we use loving speech, we avoid misunderstanding and much suffering. Even if other people use harsh language when talking to us, we will suffer less if we use only loving speech in return. When we have understanding and compassion, we have lightness and we can communicate well with other people, even those who are violent and cruel. We can accept them; we know they are unhappy and that they are victims of their own anger, violence, and discrimination. When compassion and understanding are in us, we are no longer motivated by the desire for punishment or revenge. Loving speech becomes available to us and communication becomes possible.

Without real communication, happiness can't exist. To be surrounded by family, friends, and a spiritual community that know how to use loving speech is a great daily blessing. Because happiness is possible here on Earth, the Buddha often spoke of practical blessings such as this.

> *"To be able to serve and support your parents,*
> *To cherish your own family,*
> *To have a vocation that brings you joy—*
> *This is the greatest happiness."*

Your parents are the ones who raised you and cared for you when you were little. Now that you are an adult, you can support your parents as they supported you. That is the highest blessing. There are many ways to support parents. We can offer financial support if we have that resource, but we can also offer spiritual and emotional support. Financial offerings are wonderful; however, more people suffer spiritually than financially. If we know how to practice and keep the mindfulness trainings, then we become a pillar of our family, able to support them in times of suffering and difficulty.

A long monastic history demonstrates this point. Although monastics don't hold jobs in the secular world and don't have money to send home to their parents, if they practice diligently, with equanimity and happiness, they are able to help many people and their family also benefits from this. In difficult times, they can be spiritual leaders, bringing reconciliation to their families.

A monk who practices successfully becomes the spiritual leader in his family, even though he may be very young. When a monastic opens her heart to intervene, her brothers, sisters, aunts, and uncles listen to her because she represents a source of spiritual love.

We do not need to become monastics to have this role in our families. If we use loving speech, let go of our attachment to outcomes, and base our acts on compassion and love instead of anger and jealousy, we can become pillars of support for our families.

As a practitioner, our aim is not to make a lot of money. Our aim is to transform the suffering in our heart, to live in equanimity, peace, and happiness, and to offer happiness to our family and those around us.

Our happiness multiplies exponentially when we see that we can bring happiness to those around us. This is reality, not superstition. In a retreat of five hundred people, there may be hundreds of them who come back to thank us after they have practiced. We can see the transformation in them. As each of us becomes more at ease and more aware of our capacity to love, we are more able to reconcile with our families and our loved ones if there has been conflict. Easing a long conflict with a loved one is a great source of happiness right in that very moment. We don't need to wait ten years to reap the happiness that is the fruit of our practice.

> *"To live honestly, generous in giving,*
> *To offer support to relatives and friends,*
> *Living a life of blameless conduct—*
> *This is the greatest happiness."*

"To live honestly" is to act virtuously, to be just, and to offer ourselves to life. To be generous is not simply to share our money, material resources, and technical knowledge; generosity does not require money. The offering of wealth, goods, or knowledge is only one of the many forms of generosity. There is a second form of generosity, offering the Dharma. We can always offer and model the way to practice to alleviate suffering. This offering is much more precious than the financial offering. Most precious is the third kind of offering, the gift of non-fear, *abhaya*. The greatest gift in life is to live without fear and to teach others to do so as well. The offering of material goods, of the Dharma, and of non-fear are gifts from Avalokiteshvara Bodhisattva.

Many people are victims of their fear. If we can alleviate someone's fear, that is the greatest gift that we can offer them. Our life will be filled with happiness if we can help others around us. But if we spend our whole life building up our name and our fortune, then we cannot find happiness. We might have a lot of money, a big house, a luxurious car, but that's not real happiness. We can only taste real happiness when we can help others around us. And we have to start with those in our family and the dear friends around us. We have to help family, relatives, and friends first before we are capable of helping others outside our circle. If we're successful in helping our brothers and sisters in the Sangha, then we definitely will be able to help our loved ones. If, in our daily life, we can't help our brothers and sisters, then how can we offer help to others? We have to be successful in helping the people around us alleviate their suffering. That is the highest blessing, and that blessing has a lasting effect.

To be able to act without regret is a source of great happiness. This means we have nothing to regret in our words or actions toward others. We should be able to ask ourselves, "Have I done anything to my teacher, my friend, my father, my mother, that has made me feel regret later?" Asking this question will help us avoid any hint of regret, and will ensure that our speech and actions will not cause harm to others.

When our speech and actions cause no harm, we face a future without remorse. If we are burdened with regret, happiness is impossible. If we have erred in the past, or said something that caused harm, we can transform that past action and regret through the process of Beginning Anew.[15] We can commit ourselves to acting and speaking peacefully in the future, and then lasting happiness will again be available to us. If we can transform our mind and be determined not to say things or act in ways that will cause regret, then our mind will be cleansed and become luminous, and all the mistakes and errors of the past will completely disappear.

This is practicing according to the teaching of the Buddha. The errors originated in our mind, and when we transform our mind, we have the determination to refrain from committing the same errors in the future. When we transform our mind, we are immediately cleansed. The guilt we feel is lifted and the dark past disappears. This is called the practice of Beneficial Regret and Beginning Anew. Only when we're determined to make a vow to ourselves and our Sangha that we will not commit such acts or speak such words, can our error and our guilt be lifted. But this requires a strong determination and our determination won't be strong if we don't make this vow in front of both our Sangha and the Buddha.

Thus, kneeling down to prostrate, practicing Beginning Anew, and taking the Five Mindfulness Trainings with determination and resolve, will instantly make our guilt from the past disappear. When the mind is no longer loaded with guilt, then the guilt no longer exists. That's the principle of Beneficial Regret and Beginning Anew in Buddhism, being able to act without a hint of guilt. In English we can also call it "blameless conduct."

"To avoid unwholesome actions,
Not caught by alcoholism or drugs,
And to be diligent in doing good things—
This is the greatest happiness."

Our society is organized in such a way that it creates lonely people by the tens of thousands every day. And when we carry such despair and loneliness within us, it creates a vacuum. We feel compelled to fill that vacuum and forget our suffering with drugs, alcohol, careless sex, and the kind of entertainment that destroys our bodies and minds. Guns, armies, and prisons can't solve the problem of drugs and alcohol. The only way to ease this sense of emptiness and loneliness is to create an environment where young people can live joyfully. And if we ourselves don't live joyfully, we can't help our children or provide them with a good environment either.

Any speech, act, or thought that we feel might cause harm to others or to ourselves, is unwholesome. Even a joke that causes others to suffer or hurts their feelings is unwholesome. Not only do the victims suffer, but the perpetrators also share the suffering. Though others can't read your mind, you still suffer from negative thoughts. You may suffer tremendously, even if you're the only one who knows it.

Anything that clouds our mind is considered an intoxicant, whether it is drugs, alcohol, or gossip. We consume these intoxicants thinking that they will make us happy, but only when our minds are clear does happiness truly become available to us.

We should also be diligent in doing good deeds. If there's any work that can bring happiness to ourselves or to others, we should do it without hesitation. Even when work benefits others, we too taste the fruit of happiness from it. These good deeds are blessings, and the happiness that comes from doing them will surely follow.

> *"To be humble and polite in manner,*
> *To be grateful and content with a simple life,*
> *Not missing the occasion to learn the Dharma—*
> *This is the greatest happiness."*

To be humble means that you don't put yourself above somebody else. We can learn to be humble and to have reverence for all others, even when they are younger than we are. A young child deserves to be treated with humility and respect.

Young children often invoke a true sense of contentment and gratitude, for they are content with very little. A stick can provide hours of joy and entertainment to a child. In order to be happy, we have to learn to live simply. When we live simply, we have much more time and we can be in touch with the many wonders of life. Living simply is the criterion for the new culture, the new civilization. With the development of technology, people lead more and more complicated lives. Shopping has replaced other activities as our mode for satisfying ourselves. The criterion for being happy is to live simply and to have harmony and peace in yourself and between yourself and the people around you, without aggressiveness, irritation, and anger. We must know the limit, we must know how much is enough. This is the antidote for wanting more and more and more. You know what is sufficient, what is enough for you.

There is a Vietnamese proverb, "Tri tuc, tien tuc, dai tuc, ha thoi tuc." That means, settling for "good enough" is enough. If we wait until all our needs and wants are met, we may wait forever. "Tri tuc" means "good enough." "Good enough" means being content with the minimum amount necessary. Your shirt and pair of shoes can last another year. It's all right for three or four people to share a desk for studying, there's no need for each to have her own desk. Settling for "good enough" in terms of simple living will bring us contentment, satisfaction, and happiness immediately. As long as we think our lives are not good enough, we will not have happiness. As soon as we realize our lives are good enough, happiness immediately appears. That is the practice of contentment.

In Vietnam there's a school of Buddhism called the Four Gratitudes. Just by practicing gratitude, we can find happiness. We must be grateful to our ancestors, our parents, our teachers, our friends, the Earth, the sky, the trees, the grass, the animals, the soil, the stones. Looking at the sunlight or at the forest, we feel gratitude. Looking at our breakfast, we feel gratitude. When we live in the spirit of gratitude, there will be much happiness in our life. The one who is grateful is the one who has much happiness, while the one who is ungrateful will not be able to have happiness.

If someone offers you a teaching, a Dharma talk, take it. Seize any opportunity to learn the Dharma. A Dharma talk is not a lecture, but an opportunity to open ourselves up and allow the deepest levels of our consciousness to be penetrated and nourished by the Dharma. Listening to a Dharma talk can take the misunderstanding and ignorance out of us. It can take away our craving, anger, and hatred. The more toxins we remove, the more our hearts will feel light and free, and happiness will be possible. Happiness grows from inside out.

Those who conduct their life according to this principle will have lasting happiness.

> *"To persevere and be open to change,*
> *To have regular contact with monks and nuns,*
> *And to fully participate in Dharma discussions—*
> *This is the greatest happiness."*

When we can yield to reason and let someone correct us without becoming angry or resentful, then we will find that happiness remains with us. It is incredibly difficult, but when our brothers and our sisters point out our faults, the best thing we can do is put our palms together and bow in appreciation, with graciousness on our faces and in our hearts.

The benefit in being close to a monk or nun is the opportunity to learn the Dharma. That is why young men and women like to hang around monks and nuns at the temple. This is a very great blessing!

A Dharma discussion is an opportunity to express ourselves and to listen and learn from others. We can share our joys, difficulties, insights, experiences, and questions. Using loving speech and deep listening, we can also focus on important matters of concern, such as how to create a good environment for our children, our children's children, our larger community, and the Earth as a whole.

"To live diligently and attentively,

To perceive the Noble Truths,

And to realize nirvana—

This is the greatest happiness."

To live diligently and attentively means walking, standing, lying down, sitting, working, eating and doing everything in mindfulness.

The Four Noble Truths are at the heart of Buddhist practice[16]. Thanks to the Four Noble Truths, we will be able to practice and realize nirvana. Nirvana is something very concrete, the absence of afflictions and the presence of solidity, freedom, and wellbeing. To realize nirvana is to be completely liberated and cease all suffering while we are living in the world. All afflictions are dissolved, and only perfect equanimity remains. This is the full definition of happiness.

Because we've planted good seeds in the past, we now have the opportunity to live among the sages. In a good environment it's easy for us to plant good seeds—seeds of peace, joy, community, and happiness.

Today we are blessed to be able to sit in the middle of a healthy Sangha that practices with diligence and with ease; we are reaping the benefit of the good seeds we have planted in the past. We need to continue our path and not abandon our good environment.

> *"To live in the world*
> *With your heart undisturbed by the world,*
> *With all sorrows ended, dwelling in peace—*
> *This is the greatest happiness."*

Although we are still living in this mundane world, our minds can be imperturbable. We don't need to be flustered by all that we see and hear. The practice of letting go is essential for our happiness. We distance ourselves from the influences that destroy our body and mind, so that we are able to release the many worries and concerns that consume us and prevent us from getting in touch with the wonders of life that we need for our nourishment. There are many things we cannot let go of, and so we miss the opportunity to get in touch with what is more important, and with what is refreshing and healing that is always available to us. We get caught in a kind of prison. Recognizing that these worries and concerns are not really important, we are able to release them, and suddenly happiness comes right away.

It's like when you leave the city behind to go to the countryside. It may take forty-five minutes or an hour to get out of the city, and when the hills begin to appear and the breeze begins to caress your face, you feel so happy because you've been able to leave the city behind you. All of us have had this kind of experience.

Have you ever met someone who seems to be skilled in the art of letting go? A friend or a teacher can remind us and help us let go of worry, craving, and concern, so we can be free to encounter the wonders of life that are in the here and the now. If we see someone living in this world who is not disturbed by the ebb and flow of life, not enmeshed in afflictions, that person has freedom, that person is solid. To see such a person is the highest blessing. When we master this quality, all of our worldly afflictions dissolve and we become indestructible, completely at peace. We can become that person by practicing happiness in the present moment.

> *"For the one who accomplishes this*
> *Is unvanquished wherever she goes;*
> *Always he is safe and happy—*
> *Happiness lives within oneself."*

The World-honored One has said that we should not predict the future based on what happened in the past. We need to base the future on our own actions in the present. Our actions are our karma, and so are our thoughts, our speech, our intentions, and our attitude. If we live in the Dharma, we can generate our own blessings. Our happiness is a lasting one that can be carried on to the next life. We can find happiness no matter what situation we might be thrown into.

Wherever we may go, we will feel the secure protection of the Dharma. Wherever we may go, we will feel strong and solid. The solidity comes from the practice. The greatest blessing is not the one that falls down from the sky and is handed to us. The greatest blessing is the happiness that each of us can generate for ourselves.

NOTES

1. This sutra was translated from Pali in Chinese by the Parthian monk, An Shih Kao, at the Lo Yang Center in China during the later Han dynasty (140–171 CE). The ancient form of this sutra is the culmination of several smaller works combined. The sutra is entirely in accord with both the Mahayana and Theravada traditions of Buddhism.
2. The four elements are earth, air, water, and fire.
3. The five skandhas are forms, feelings, perceptions, mental formations, and consciousness.
4. A bodhisattva, "awakening being," is someone committed to enlightening oneself and others so that all may be liberated from suffering.

5. The four kinds of Mara are unwholesome mental factors, five skandhas, death, and distractions (e.g., fantasies or forgetfulness).
6. The three worlds are desire and passion, form (without desire and passion), and formlessness (only mental functioning).
7. The five desires are being wealthy, being beautiful, being ambitious, finding pleasure in eating, and being lazy.
8. Dharmakaya means the body of the teaching of awakening.
9. Nirvana is liberation from birth and death.
10. The Four Noble Truths are suffering, the cause of suffering, the end of suffering, and the Eightfold Path.
11. Dependent origination (Sanskrit, *pratitya samutpada)* means that any phenomenon arises and exists not on its own, but in a mutually interdependent web of cause and effect with all other phenomena.
12. See Endnote 7.

13. The Four Foundations of Mindfulness are body, feeling, state of mind, and mental contents.
14. The Mangala Sutta, sometimes called the Mahamangala Sutta, appears in the Suttanipata and in the Khuddakapatha. It also appears in the Jataka (tales of the Buddha's earlier births, often in animal-fable form).
15. For the Beginning Anew Ceremony, see Thich Nhat Hanh, *Chanting from the Heart* (Berkeley, CA: Parallax Press, 2006). [Formerly *The Plum Village Chanting and Recitation Book* (Parallax Press, 2000).
16. See Endnote 10.

Dharmacharya Shantum Seth, a teacher ordained by Thich Nhat Hanh, offers teachings and shares the practice of Mindfulness meditation in different parts of India and the world. He also leads pilgrimages, 'In the Footsteps of the Buddha'.

Please visit: www.buddhapath.com or contact info@buddhapath.com

Ahimsa Trust represents Thich Nhat Hanh and his community in India. It is a volunteer driven, non-profit trust, working to create peace, in one's self and in the world. Ahimsa Trust organizes Days of Mindfulness and retreats/workshops across India, especially for educators.

Please visit www.ahimsatrust.org or contact ahimsa.trust@gmail.com

For worldwide contacts and teachings of Thich Nhat Hanh and his community, please visit www.plumvillage.org